TOOLS &
TECHNOLOGY
IN THE
DIGITAL AGE

Howard Tullman

BLOG
into**BOOK**

Published in the United States of America
For bulk orders, please contact info@blogintobook.com

Cover design portrait courtesy of Matthew Cherry
Perspiration Principles logo designed by James "Red" Schmitt
Special Thanks to Lakshmi Shenoy and Claudia Saric

To purchase all volumes of The Perspiration Principles, please visit:
BlogIntoBook.com/tullman/

ISBN: 9781619849792

DEDICATION

Sitting down every week to write something that will be meaningful and ideally of lasting value to others is a lot like setting out to start a new business. Sometimes there's a germ of an idea; sometimes it's an emotional reaction or other driver; or perhaps it's just a problem or situation that needs to be addressed. And occasionally you simply want to see things change and no one else is stepping up to the plate to make that happen.

You can't know how hard, long or costly (in many ways) the journey will be and there are no guarantees that anything good will ever come of your efforts, but you know for certain that nothing will ever happen if you don't get the process started and try. It's a lonely path and every bit of encouragement, assistance and support that you find along the way makes the job a little easier and slightly more likely to succeed.

I hope that these books will be my modest contribution to your success and to the well-worn and tattered bag of hopes and dreams which we call entrepreneurship.

CONTENTS

TECHNOLOGY IS A TOOL, NOT A SOLUTION

I have consistently said (for longer than I care to remember) that, at least for me, there's a really simple test to evaluate the viability of an idea for a new B-to-B business. Does the proposed product or service save the end user time; does it save the customer or client money; or does it increase their productivity? If so, let's talk further. If not, take your plan and take a hike.

Now I understand that there are ideas for businesses that are intended to address other social objectives and that you can't measure those kinds of endeavors solely by their financial bottom line, but that's not what I'm talking about here. And frankly, those types of businesses are not representative of the vast majority of the proposals that I see every day. So, while there are clear exceptions to every set of rules, I'm sticking with my 3 simple questions until someone shows me a better approach.

And, of course, the ultimate dream is to find a business that does all of the above. It's not really as hard as it sounds especially today when new technologies are ripping through every old line traditional industry and turning things upside down. I see businesses every day that are disrupting the old ways of doing business simply by taking steps, obstacles and costs out of the old way that things have been done forever and dragging those businesses into the new world.

And what is so interesting to me is that the lion's share of the opportunities and new solutions (medical technologies are an exception) don't necessarily involve newly invented or untested technologies – they are nothing more than cases of smart people applying proven and industrial strength technologies to eliminate waste and inefficiencies and improve outcomes. This is the critical difference between invention and innovation. Innovation is smarter, faster, less expensive and less risky than trying to invent the next big thing from whole cloth. Good technology is necessary for great products and services, but it's not sufficient in itself to get the job done.

The new and inexpensive technologies which are now available pretty much everywhere are certainly enablers of the digital revolution (as is the rise of mobility and constant connectivity) and these tools make the process improvements and new solutions feasible and cost-effective, but it remains true that the real drivers of disruptive change are always the same: entrepreneurs (who probably didn't know what "couldn't" be done) and who look at things that everyone else has seen for years, but think something new and different and then go on to build something that changes the whole ball game.

Amazingly enough, once you have the cutting insight that changes everyone's perspective of whatever problem you're trying to solve, you discover that the "app" or the new technology is a conduit that is helpful in the process, but it's generally not the central reason for the appeal and attractiveness of the new approach. A good example is *Snapsheet* which is using mobile technologies (phones and cameras) to change the way that insurance adjusters do their work. Consumers simply use the *Snapsheet* app to take a series of photos of the damage to their car and upload it to *Snapsheet* where a room full of experienced adjusters immediately evaluates the damage and determines how the loss should be handled. Losses can be settled in hours rather than days or weeks. And that's just the beginning.

Snapsheet is one of those rare companies that are delivering a beneficial solution to auto insurance companies across all 3 of my test vectors. Time, money and productivity.

(1) Save Me Time

Claimants get settlements in hours. They don't have to waste time sitting around their house waiting for an adjuster to show up. The adjuster doesn't waste his time (and half a day) driving all over the city to look at a fender bender. In addition, using readily-available data, adjusters can instantly determine based on the age and mileage of the damaged vehicle whether any repair is appropriate or whether they should just "total" the car and write a check on the spot.

(2) Save Me Money

Insurers save boatloads of money avoiding the costs of providing rental cars for their insureds. Transportation and fuels costs shrink dramatically. Faster settlements have less unhappy parties and significantly fewer supplementary payments.

(3) Increase My Productivity

Adjusters can process far more claims every day because they aren't wasting travel time and gas on useless trips. In addition, they're sitting in a room surrounded by other expert adjusters instead of being The Lone Ranger standing out in some cornfield or driveway trying to write an estimate. Faster, better, more accurate and fully documented transactions mean happier insureds and employees as well.

But the thing that is so striking is that the major benefits from using *Snapsheet* don't really arise from the "app" or the underlying technology – any mobile device that can capture and send images could get the job done – the real value arises from smart (and now obvious) improvements in the efficiency of the adjusting process. This is why the best businesses don't lead with their technology – they lead with solution selling addressed to known and obvious problems.

WHY DIGITAL WINS

I have to laugh and just shake my head when people tell me that they are working on the digital strategy for their business or reluctantly ask me to help them figure out what they should be doing about social media as if it's a new form of head lice or psoriasis or something equally disgusting, contagious and unavoidable. It's a little like saying that you've decided you're going to spend a little time each day breathing – even though you're pretty busy with a bunch of other commitments – because it seems like the smart thing to do.

Digital technologies and social media channels and the new degrees and depth of "connection" that they enable are so mission-critical these days and so pervade every aspect of what we need to be doing in our lives and companies – as every business in the world migrates rapidly from analog anything to digital everything – that the incorporation of these powerful tools and technologies isn't an option or a choice, they are inevitable additions to your arsenal and, frankly, the sooner the better. I see the two alternative paths as very binary – you can engage or you can be extinct. Change and grow or die – pretty stark choices. You can face the facts or you can be like that lonesome old fax machine sitting in the corner just dreading the day when it will finally be unplugged and trashed.

This is a major topic which is well-suited for a series of columns, but, for the moment, I just want to give you a short list of the 5 major dimensions of enablement which digital is bringing to the game. If you ask yourself what you are doing or about to do in your business to take advantage of these new resources, tools, technologies, channels and perspectives which are now available basically because of the digital datafication of everything, you'll get a head start on your peers and competitors. It's not an easy process or a short path, but it's already well underway and you need to get with the program or get left behind. It's always the same story: you can make the dust or you can eat someone else's dust.

One crucial aspect of this ongoing and highly-disruptive transformation which the mass media really doesn't seem to appreciate is that the most critical attribute of the Internet is NOT its immediacy or its low cost; it is the heightened direct access to identified individuals, the ability to accurately measure and react to their ongoing engagement in real time, and the media spend direction and accountability that it enables.

Here are the 5 vital vectors:

(1) Superior Customer Targeting and Offer Optimization

I've talked before about hyper-personalization (customer demographics) which morphed quickly into determining and tracking interests and attitudes (customer preferences and desires) and now we're moving forward again to anticipatory actions which let us drive and leverage future customer behaviors. This is a page right out of the canon of Steve Jobs who basically said that consumers don't know what they want until we create it and show it to them. Or as Henry Ford might have said about consumer demand for the Model T: If I had asked people at the time what they wanted, they would have said they needed faster horses, not automobiles.

(2) New Levels of Analytics & Insights Based on Speed & Scale

Size is nice, but in today's world, speed is what kills. It's not the big guys who are moving the needle today; it's the fast and responsive guys. Everything we're doing today in marketing is time-compressed and the rate of required change continues to accelerate. You'll never see smart marketers buying 12 week campaigns any longer and then sitting back and hoping things work out well. We have tools to see how things are trending in our campaigns on a minute-to-minute basis and today that's the standard for reacting to those behaviors as well. We're not talking about an A/B testing world any more. We're talking about A to Z systems that can launch 20 alternative offers to a small (and inexpensive, but representative) segment of a target list; collect and collate the responses in real time (minutes rather than months); prioritize the winning pitches and kill off the losers and then launch the winners against the larger lists and continue this iterative process all day long. No one said it was gonna be easy – just essential. And the ante just keeps getting upped.

If you haven't seen and started to use GOOGLE Product Listing Ads (PLAs), you're late. But what's most important is to understand – not how much more appealing a GOOGLE search response is which features multiple responsive product images and pricing from local merchants – you need to appreciate how much more work this represents for each local merchant. Every product has to be imaged, catalogued, loaded and priced (realistically, the pricing almost needs to be dynamic for your particular offerings to remain competitive) and the whole thing needs to be actively managed and updated constantly. It's a whole every day job just to stay in the game and increasingly it's going to have to be machine-driven and informed – much like programmed stock trading. But who's going to create and supply these kinds of tools for SMBs to permit them to remain competitive in these new, high-speed marketplaces? I see this whole area as just another amazing set of opportunities for entrepreneurs. But even if you're not building the new tools for the rest of us, you'd better be doing something in your business to respond.

(3) Ability to Change Consumer Behaviors in Real Time

If you're always reacting (regardless of how quickly) to the behavior of the consumers you're trying to reach, in today's world of high-velocity computing, you'll always be behind the curve and behind your competition because the game is now to get ahead of the consumer and to "know before they go" so that you can be there when they arrive. Sites like www.chango.com offer these kinds of tools for smart marketers with response and reaction times in the area of 10 milliseconds – faster than a webpage can load. As you can imagine, if I'm taking search results (what you found) and I'm trying to launch offers to you in response to those searches, I'm going to <u>always</u> lose out to the competitors whose tools and technologies enable them to determine what I'm looking for and present me with those choices rather than waiting for me to ask or find the answers on my own. It's a world moving from diagnostics (historical analysis) to prognostics (anticipation and prediction) and you need to get your business on the bus or you'll be left behind.

(4) Two-Way Channels for Ongoing Consumer Conversations

The ability to have ongoing, long-term, unmediated and bi-directional conversations with our customers on a massive scale provides us with the tools and channels we need to increase the lifetime value of each customer (LCV). Nothing is more directly connected to profitability than growing your share of each of your customers' spend and improving your retention of those customers. You now have the ability to determine - not simply whether your customers are seeing or hearing your messages, but whether they are listening to them and responding to them in meaningful ways. We've moved from a broadcast world (call it "spray and pray") to improved and more targeted unilateral communications and now we're moving forward again to two-way talks and credible conversations.

(5) Concrete and Readily Available Metrics – CAC, CSI, CRM

Data is the Oil of the Digital Age. If you don't already understand how critical access to and the constant measurement of the data which drives your business has become to your survival (not simply your success), there's not much I can add to the discussion. As Louis Armstrong used to say: "If you have to ask what jazz is, you'll never know".

FIND ME A FLYWHEEL TO MAKE ME A FORTUNE

I've seen the future and it's a flywheel. Not a physical flywheel, but a system that – for all intents and purposes – is actually its more expansive and digital equivalent. A system that replaces the momentum which a flywheel creates and gathers as it spins and accelerates with the expansive digital power which we have come to call the "network effect". Actually, my favorite flywheel these days isn't a physical or digital object at all – it's a relatively new, second-generation (or maybe a third generation) ad tech startup business based in New York which is called *Simple Reach* (www. simplereach.com) and which has built tools and a measurement/ content distribution platform that permits publishers and brands to make much more effective and intelligent use of all of the branded and sponsored content they are creating to help them burnish their brands and better connect at a higher level with their customers.

The network effect (which was first formulated by George Gilder and is now generally known as Metcalfe's Law) is basically a description of the expanding value of a communications network as it adds additional nodes or links. The rate of growth in the intrinsic value of the network is not linear, but exponential and multiplies ever faster as the network expands. What *Simple Reach* has done is create an enterprise model where its customers themselves (as well as interested third parties who may be prospective customers) increasingly help build *SR*'s business and grow its user and customer base (without any direct compensation) mainly because it serves their own selfish and competitive interests to do so. There's no more authentic and convincing promoter and marketer for your business than a satisfied customer who makes it his or her business to invite more people to the party. That's the flywheel in action.

Why do they do this?

First because it dramatically increases the value of the *SR* tools and services for each of them in their own businesses. You can never go wrong counting on smart business people to act in their own self-interest. From the brand's standpoint, each new publisher added to the *SR* reporting network increases the brand's ability to more fully measure – in a unified and standardized manner – the value and impact of its spending on a given campaign. From the publisher's standpoint, each new brand added to the program (by the publisher or independently by *SR*) which then has the ability to extend its ongoing and new campaigns and its marketing spend to that publisher's channels creates more revenue opportunities and more of a one-stop solution set for the publisher.

And second, because the publishers (and frankly the agencies as well) really have no choice but to adopt such a system because their own customers are starting to demand that they use the *SR* methodology and provide them with the results which they can then readily fold into their own analysis. Sometimes a given brand will have learned about the *Simple Reach* service from a different use case with a different publisher (or obviously from *SR* itself – although they do very little sales or marketing right now – relying mainly on word-of-mouth and cross-referrals) and then – in discussions with other publishers, the brand will expect and often specify this type of data and reporting and make it clear that – if such support is not available – it will be pleased to take its business elsewhere.

Frankly, no publisher today can afford to be without these kinds of offerings which are really the newest and most powerful windows to the digital world.

And finally, because, if the middle men (publishers or agencies) don't provide these services to their customers (the brands), the customers will go right around them directly to *Simple Reach* and sign up for the services. And, as it happens, that's already beginning to happen as the ultimate brand customers start to understand that they need these tools for all their marketing channels and not simply for the initial channel (or agency or publisher) which may have brought the *SR* service to their attention. Frankly, the brands already see themselves more and more as content publishers anyway and so it's a simple step (no pun intended) to contract directly for these kinds of resources – especially when – as noted above - they provide constantly more efficient one-stop shopping and integrated surveillance and tracking dashboards.

This is the kind of growth engine that you want to hang your hat on and then hold on tight for the rapid ride. And it's the kind that's very hard to come by and, as often as not, may end up flying off the track and throwing everyone for a loss. But if you find the right engine in the right marketplace and environment and your guy is the first player there, then the extent of the potential upside is hard to imagine.

It's not simply that (a) pervasive and truly additive platforms – once in place – are almost impossible to dislodge and (b) that increasingly technology spaces are becoming more and more "winner take all" plays; it's that the momentum and the earning potential accelerates at such an overwhelmingly rapid pace that even the biggest players can't respond quickly enough to the new competitive threat or use their size and resources effectively to offset the early advantages of the growing cash cushion of the first mover.

Especially in the case of a new business, that cash cushion provides several layers of comfort and security. First, management can focus on the business, not on what often – in new growing businesses - feels like perpetual fundraising. Second, early mistakes are less likely to threaten the business's existence since the business can pivot if necessary without payroll becoming a problem. Third, the customers are comforted by the bankroll and much less concerned about betting their business on the newest kid in town. Fourth, the company can afford to support simultaneous pilots and trials for far more customers than most startups. And finally, there's very little pressure on the pricing of the business's services since the company doesn't have to engage in price cutting in order to win new accounts.

But there's an even more powerful factor at work in cases like this and it's the "lock-in" investment (not in terms of dollars, but in terms of tangible business benefits) which creates powerful barriers and overwhelming switching costs even for those clients and customers which are willing to consider any kind of shift or movement. Both of these considerations are not matters of dollars and sense; they are concerns that anyone attempting to switch and losing even a moment's time or presence in these fiercely competitive marketplaces would be irreparably damaged and disadvantaged to such an extent that any such considerations would never be worth the risk.

As a result, flywheel businesses enjoy another interesting benefit – the customers seek out and readily agree to multi-year contracts - which is somewhat counter-intuitive when you are dealing with new, young companies until you realize just how quickly these kinds of new data services become mission-critical to the customers and just how addictive and additive they can be. The customers (who ordinarily would be reluctant to make longer-term commitments to a startup) quickly start to attempt to sign multi-year agreements for two reasons: (1) they become concerned about the startup's overall capacity to meet the growing demand for its offerings and they want to be sure that their own needs will continue to be met; and (b) as they incorporate the new company's products and services into their own businesses, they want to be sure that the company sticks around and stays in business.

As long as the startup retains the ability over time to continue to raise its prices and otherwise adapt and improve its products and services, this is nothing but great news for the new business because it creates unexpected levels of stability, predictable future revenue streams, and assurances that the company's future is sufficiently secure that it can make appropriate growth plans and also attract first-class talent to what would otherwise appear to be a far riskier opportunity.

So what does all this say about the future of content marketing (which continues to grow like crazy as the big brand advertisers try to create viable and continuing substantive/emotional connections with their customers) and what do you need to be thinking about for your business as you try to determine how to most profitably spend your digital marketing resources?

First, it's important to understand that we are moving into the second generation of the digital marketing revolution. If the first generation was the brute force ability to get your material (content) and your associated messages out and in front of the digital consumer (on every device), the second generation is all about tracking and measuring the efficacy and amplification of those efforts and getting better at getting it out there all the time. It's no longer about tonnage – it's all about transparency and touching the right targets at the right time in order to deliver the appropriate information and incentives to them.

Second, especially in the media/publishing marketplace, accountability is now the be-all and the end-all. No one takes your word for anything these days – no matter how much wine you pour down them - it's a "show me or see ya" world and the winners are the ones with the documentation and the ammunition to make their cases. If you can't convincingly connect spend to traffic to engagement (and organic sharing) and ultimately to conversions and concrete results, you really can't compete for much longer in this space.

We know most of these initiatives won't work, but we need to know which are working and which aren't as soon as possible so we can tactically adjust the aggregate dollar spend in order to optimize our dollars and our results. The old idea that you would simply "set it and forget it"; spend ratably the same amounts across various campaign channels; and sit back and wait for the results might have been the only way to go in the old days before we had real time responses and metrics, but it's a lazy and stupid strategy today.

And even discussing the best post-campaign documentation feels a lot like too little and too late because it's fundamentally about after-the-fact analysis and not utilizing ongoing actionable insights. The best players are focused on prognosis (prediction and real-time adjustment) rather than diagnosis which is basically all about looking backwards to see what worked. You want to be able to shift the sands under the consumers' feet and up the ante when you see where it makes sense to increase the spending behind already successful sharing in order to press your bet, amplify the impact, and increase the return on your initial investment in the development, creation and delivery of that content.

And so, in this newest media world, the real winners will be the ones who can not only help their clients track and measure effectiveness in real-time, but whose tools permit immediately take the next and most critical actions to accelerate and double down on what is working before these fleeting opportunities pass them by. It's an old venture capital rule of thumb – you feed your winners and you starve your losers. And that's where the guys at *Simple Reach* really come into their own as their rapid growth and multi-line expansion are showing. As I always say, you want to be there when the customer wants to buy and *Simple Reach* helps its clients track and get the right messages in front of the right customers in order to reach them at the right moment – when they are receptive and ready to buy.

It's that simple (no pun intended), but it's not easy and these guys are simply crushing it.

LOOK FOR LEAPFROGGING, NOT LINEAR, ADVANCES

Too much of our planning for growth these days is predicated on incremental improvements, brand extensions, product re-sizing, territorial expansions and the like. These are attempts to capture market share available in readily-apparent adjacencies rather than through undertaking new journeys and adventures and they're generally safe and sound bets for big companies. One problem with this approach is that these are paths and choices that are demonstrably evolutionary rather than revolutionary – they're great add-ons, but rarely will they generate needle-moving numbers. Sure bets guarantee small margins. The standard "no one ever got fired" process is all about taking carefully-qualified steps forward instead of making quantum leaps.

But it's becoming increasingly clear that this heads-down, "grind it out" approach (which might have been entirely prudent and reasonable in less flush or chaotic times) keeps many of us from seeing and seizing certain kinds of disruptive and game-changing opportunities which are being enabled today primarily by the rapid spread and availability of new low-cost technologies and by the dual explosion of ubiquitous mobility and connectivity. If we are principally focused on getting as close as possible to achieving our currently defined goals and objectives (and our operating numbers for the quarter or the year), it's just not very likely that we're going to look beyond those targets and over the horizon in order to see the less obvious and more extraordinary areas of possible change.

The truth is that we just don't have to do things in the same calculated and mechanical ways that we always have in the past and we especially don't have to construct the kinds of capital-intensive, costly and time-consuming foundations (including, but not limited to, every kind of bricks and mortar solution that is out there today) which were required and essential supports in the past, but which today simply constrain us and slow us down. This isn't simply that old familiar conversation to the effect that "we didn't need better buggy whips or faster horses, we needed cars"; it's an even broader commentary than that. We don't need the horses, we don't need the stables, and, frankly, any day now, we may not need the drivers themselves.

What we need is new inspiration and new approaches that are disruptive and discontinuous – not linear extensions – but true experiments with admittedly unknown outcomes and results, but which also represent the prospect of exponential potential gains. And the very good news today is that these types of new solutions can be implemented in less costly ways than ever before so that the real risks and downsides of continued experimentation can be constrained and largely mitigated.

It's also encouraging to see that these innovative approaches aren't limited to new businesses, but are being incorporated in the strategies of plenty of large and old line companies as well. Admittedly, in some cases, they are acting belatedly and defensively rather than leading the charge, but at least they are moving in the right direction. But whatever the age and size of your business, you need to be thinking about the steps you should be taking to distance and differentiate your products and services from both the competition you can see today and the much more threatening and extensive competition still to come. And, even more importantly, you need to ask yourself what – if anything – is the sustainable competitive advantage that you are hoping to create for your business so that it can compete in the future on anything other than price which is always a race to the bottom for any business.

No one can tell you the specific steps you will need to take to make these jumps, but here are two interesting and instructive cases which are worth continuing to watch in order to see how they might be applicable to your own situation. One is a done deal and one is an open question.

(1) The Book Biz is About Anything But Books

Please don't call anyone in the book biz a "publisher" these days just because – if you twist their arms – they might sell you a book. The "P" word is definitely out and the new industry buzzwords are all about adaptive learning and learning management systems, etc. Why is this seemingly semantic change so interesting? Because – for all intents and purposes – it reflects the decisions made by all of the biggest book publishers in the land to just throw in the towel and pretty much leapfrog right over the digital book business without even trying to explore those kinds of content offerings. It would appear that they're leaving the field wide open for Amazon and Apple, but maybe they know something that isn't obvious to the rest of us. There may not be any there there any longer.

If you ask them why they didn't aggressively pursue the protected digital distribution of their content, it turns out that their decisions weren't really based on the usual considerations which continue to plague the music and film industries – theft by pirates, cheap low-quality duplication, peer-to-peer sharing, etc. It turns out that they concluded that the intrinsic value of the content itself which they had to offer was being slowly ground down to nothing by: (a) the actions of the content creators themselves (rather than the actions of others as was the case in music and movies); (b) highly-efficient used book marketers; (c) the advent of MOOCs; and (d) free webcasting of lectures and classes by universities and professors all over the world - so they just decided to jump right over the challenging and unprofitable distribution game and move to building proprietary and protectable learning systems which they could market and sell to their same customers and which would assist in teaching whatever the content might be and, more importantly, measuring the results of those efforts.

(2) A New Lease on Life for Libraries?

Libraries aren't much better off than books these days and cities and schools of every size and shape are trying to figure out what the library of the future will look like and – very frankly – what real functions it will provide which justify its continued existence and provide some kind of differentiation from so many other public and private spaces. There are about 120,000 libraries in the U.S. these days and the vast majority (pretty close to 100,000) are in schools and universities. And you can be sure that in almost every instance, there are other users, groups, departments and facility management professionals who are coveting those large (and largely empty) spaces in their institutions for a million other uses. The one thing that we know for sure is that relying on "tradition" in order to support the old ways of doing things won't do the trick much longer. Tradition these days is just a delusion of permanence and - most often – it's just an easy excuse for those who don't want to change.

So the challenge that I would leave you with is to think creatively and disruptively about what will we do with our libraries now that books are increasingly a thing of the past? Should they simply be community spaces? Safe harbors for kids after school? Coaching and supplementary education places? Or just rows and rows of recycled desktops for accessing digital everything. Right now, this is a very open question. You should regard it - not as a closed book - but as a very large volume full of empty pages.

BUILD A BRIDGE, NOT ANOTHER BAND-AID

Paul Simon and Art Garfunkel had it right and they actually didn't even know it. I think that today they'd still probably be embarrassed if someone called them "computer geeks" or said that they had perfectly articulated the newest and smartest solution we've seen in some time for the legacy and enterprise-wide computer system problems that continue to plague many of the country's largest businesses. But the fact is that they said it all in a song.

The correct solutions today (and the enormous set of opportunities they create for smart young businesses) for a great deal of the legacy leftovers, remnant and orphaned protocols, and general "spaghetti code" confusion that continues to impede important process improvements, speed and efficiency enhancements, and any amount of material innovation in these big businesses are actually pretty simple. Some of these things are sitting there in plain sight, but they're overlooked by the guys who've been staring at the same stale whiteboards for years and retreading the same tired paths. Rehashing the same old stew isn't going to help anyone get ahead.

The simple answer - as the boys used to sing in the 70's – is all about building a "bridge over troubled water". It's not about trying to implement the latest desperate attempt (in a long, sad series of stop-gap measures and bulked-up bandages) which simply adds complexity to the current code base and postpones the necessary progress to the ultimate solution. You can't save your way to these kinds of radical solutions and you can't do it on the cheap either. But you won't get anywhere at all if you don't have a new and clear vision of where you're headed.

Here's the hard truth: the guys that got them there and built the problems that these companies are living with today aren't gonna get them to the next level of solutions. They're committed to their code with their embedded approaches and they're stuck trying to drag those ancient albatrosses forward into the future. It's a heavy load; it's the wrong strategy; and it's doomed to be more of the same under the best of circumstances. There's only one way you're headed if you're looking through the rear view mirror and that's backwards.

Frankly, to solve these kinds of problems, these companies need to get help and a fresh set of uninvested eyes from the outside and they need a strategy that builds a new, streamlined and simply sufficient solution right over the top of the problems (a "bridge") rather than another massive rewriting project that takes forever, costs a fortune, moves the same deck chairs around, and basically repaints the flagpole. Even the best Band-Aid is no bargain in the long run.

And what is very interesting is that these aren't cases where the new kids on the block are going to be suggesting new things to be doing or even new ways to do them – they're creating bypasses, express lanes and other new streamlined and fast channels to get the work done. They know the inputs; they know the desired outputs and results; and they're free to determine the least costly and most efficient ways to connect them. It's as easy as that once you get over the old news.

It all comes down to a simple realization, but it's one that's very difficult for the folks whose history is closely tied to what's been built in the past to admit. They need to acknowledge that their hard work and voluminous body of code can be readily and easily replicated and, in fact, efficiently superseded by simpler and more straightforward solutions. Today it's not about the size of the effort and the lines of code created; it's about speed and throughput and – as often as not – the simpler and more elegant the code, the faster the results generated and the happier the end users.

The trick for the old guys is not to take this stuff personally. No one said that life was fair or that anything lasted forever. And the trick for good managers is to acknowledge that the rules of the game have changed and – while it's not exactly fair – it's something that needs to be recognized and lived with.

The best approach (and it's still not an easy one) is to recognize and appreciate that the guys who built the ships that got us to this point were the explorers and the trailblazers and the real inventors in many cases, but their path was long and hard and costly and full of false starts, wrong paths, broken code, etc. along with plenty of do-overs. But they still got there and that's a true accomplishment and something to be respected.

Unfortunately now for them, whether it's fair or not, the new guys with the new eyes get the easy job – they already know where the goal line is and they know what works and what the users need and now they have a much easier job – they simply need to build a bridge that spans the old code and connects the past with the future as quickly and inexpensively as possible. And that's all about execution rather than exploration and that's what it's going to take to finally break out of the restrictions and legacies of the past in order to build the paths to the future.

The way forward isn't through the morass; it's over the top.

NO ONE WINS THE RACE
TO THE BOTTOM

Today, because the barriers to entry into almost any business are so low and the costs are so modest, competitors can be in your business and in your face in an instant. And because much of the Web is still very much like the Wild West, prospects and customers have very little accurate information to go on in making their initial choices and evaluations of various products or services.

Website and service validation businesses represent an entirely new and interesting digital marketplace and Stella Service is one of the early leaders in the space trying to become the "Good Housekeeping" seal of approval for e-commerce and other sites. It's a fertile opportunity and you can bet that he'll have plenty of competition in no time at all.

But, because the need is a real one, everyone will eventually be much better served and become much smarter decision-makers by virtue of the immediate access they will have to timely and accurate comparative information concerning everything they are thinking about buying, selling, using, visiting or consuming. We're about to enter the Mocial world.

Mocial is just a mash-up of mobile and social, but what it stands for is a much more complex and important set of ideas and requirements. Mocial means providing: (1) what we need; (2) when we need it; (3) wherever we are; and (4) without asking. Places and spaces will become intelligent and active and they will tell us relevant and particularized "stories" based on who we are, where we are and what we are doing as well as our prior contextual-sensitive activities and histories. Nudge commerce and next-generation suggestive selling systems will make a lot of the basic purchase decisions for us – especially in-store or online. Google Now is an early second-generation entrant into these kinds of services

However, for the moment, as a result of inadequate and poorly distributed marketplace information, false claims and promises, bait and switch offers, and cheap prices are far too prevalent on the Web and unfortunately they're disproportionately effective for the moment. And even though price and value are two radically different things, it's often very difficult for your company to make your case in the few moments or seconds during which you typically have the buyer's attention.

Worse yet, in today's Costco-fied economy, besides price, uber-size seems to matter most to too many consumers. Measuring bigger is easy. Measuring better is much harder because it requires judgment and values. But it's not all that clear that most consumers care about long-term value especially given the highly-disposable nature and prompt obsolescence of so many of today's products and services.

As a result, you can find yourself trying to keep up with and compete against new entrants and other competitors who really have no skin in the game. Having nothing, they have nothing to lose – all they can do is mess up the market for you. And like finding a turd in the punch bowl, once the prices start to spiral down, things only get uglier and less appetizing. There's really no way back.

This is also why - for a real player - it's no fun at all to play poker for pennies. Playing for peanuts (or with people with nothing to lose) takes away the pain and pressure of making difficult choices and sacrifices. But even that's only half the story. The other reason that it's a waste of time to play for pretend stakes is that there is no real impact outside of the game if you lose. Ultimately nothing is more important to good decision-making than the ability to identify, appreciate and evaluate the costs and consequences of our actions. Not, of course, just at the poker table, but in all our business relationships and in our lives in general as well.

And please don't buy into this noise about there being room for everyone in the market and that more players just expand the overall market size. Your job is to kill the competition – if they're about to drown; throw them a nice large anvil to speed the process along. They want your family to starve and your kids to be homeless.

And even if these mopes were worthy competitors instead of low-ball artists, trying to compete on price or sheer quantity - especially for a start-up - is a very tough and risky choice and almost always a bad idea. This is why you don't wrestle with pigs – you'll both get dirty, but only the pig will enjoy it.

Not only are there no winners in the race to the lowest price, it actually turns out that, for many of us today, even "free" isn't cheap enough. This is because in many cases the costs of usage and adoption have a lot more to do with the calculated allocation of scarce personal time and precious resources rather than with just dollars and cents. In addition, there are always other and better dimensions to compete on if you're really doing your job.

So, as tough as it can sometimes be, the best plan is to ignore the guys in the cheap seats and concentrate on making sure that you're delivering a product or service that's worth the prices you're asking your customers to pay. In the end, that's all that really matters and that's what will win in the long run.

SAAS CAN BE A PAIN IN THE ASS

The promise of the cloud can be very seductive and the adoption in every industry of cloud-based solutions provided - by and large - by new, young companies offering all manner of software as a service (SaaS) solutions continues to accelerate. The prospects of reduced capital expenditures and smaller IT staffs as well as ubiquitous access and perpetual uptime are very compelling for any business.

And while I realize that there are a few big, long-established players (like Salesforce.com) in the SaaS space; if you look carefully, most of the major and more substantial players have concentrated on infrastructure plays while most of the new, interesting, and potentially highly disruptive software solutions are being offered by young players who have elected to ride on that newly available infrastructure which is inexpensive to access (though not to build) and to assemble their products and service offerings on top of these industrial-strength platforms which are being provided by Amazon, Microsoft and others.

But those new young entrants present three serious and essentially structural risks to businesses looking to move to the cloud which every CEO needs to appreciate and evaluate before making such a move. The truth is that not every "cloud" has a silver lining and – as the head of a growing company – before you bet your entire business and begin to migrate mission-critical services and offerings to the cloud - you need to be sure (a) that you really understand who you're signing up with; (b) that you appreciate what you're signing up for and what you're <u>not</u> getting; and (c) that you have an accurate picture of the risks that you are taking and how they compare to the <u>potential</u> benefits of a move. The devil is always in the details and, in many cases, the devil you know and have worked with for years (with all the warts and all the complaints) may still be a better bet for your business than a crapshoot on a company that's still getting its shit together.

Only after you get solid and complete answers to a few, very critical and important questions should you think about moving forward. These aren't easy things to determine or simple inquiries to make, but you won't get a second chance if you move prematurely or if you pick the wrong vendor/partner. You could end up entirely out of business. So take the time and commit the resources to do the necessary due diligence and to look hard before you leap. They're called "clouds" for a reason – they're not remotely transparent – they're totally opaque.

Here are some brief thoughts on the three most critical concerns and one final suggestion:

Who Are These Guys and Are Their Interests Aligned with Mine?

When you're first starting out and trying to build a new business, there's a tremendous emphasis and tons of pressure on management to keep increasing revenues. Make the sale and move on to the next. But, for the customers, the rubber really meets the road when it's implementation time and that's when the SaaS sales guys tend to be long gone. And, because installations, training, configurations and the entire process of customization for individual users don't drive "new" revenues, the senior management and top sales guys at too many of these SaaS start-ups have little or no interest in these "down and dirty", but crucial parts of the migration process. I think that this is totally because they are focused solely on the top line and compensated accordingly.

But, even if you want to give them the benefit of the doubt, and you say that – because they've never done it before – they don't understand that software development is basically a business of brief moments of creation embedded in a lifetime of maintenance; it still doesn't make life any better or smoother for their customers. Essentially the basic SaaS *modus operandi* is to sell the stuff in and then leave the rest of the work to third party consultants and integrators or to the customer. Bottom line – they're into sales, not service or support, and you can easily end up – under the best of circumstances - with a partial solution and a load of headaches.

What Am I Getting and What Do I Only "Think" I'm Getting?

Not only is the SaaS solution sometimes half-delivered; it's also often half a loaf when you look under the hood. In some ways, it's a competitive advantage to be young enough not to know any better and not to know what you can't do. Entrepreneurs regularly bite off too much and promise far more than they can deliver. Business as usual – buyer beware – no harm, no foul. But other times, especially with first-generation software programs, the initial set of buyers are involuntarily turned into the last beta testers and – believe me – that doesn't make for happy campers. In this context, I like to say that SaaS software changes and upgrades aren't released; they escape from the engineers. Newbies seize on the "lean" methodology jargon as an excuse to launch all kinds of under-cooked and half-assed products, but we're all pretty tired of hearing that flaws are actually features, and not bugs. And, in addition, it turns out that, by "lean", they don't even mean simply-designed initial MVPs;

they mean that they plan to learn what works and what doesn't by leaning on the users and letting them live through all the hiccups and mistakes.

Young entrepreneurs rarely understand the difference between a software program and a software product. Developing a robust and stable software product (with programs incorporated into it) which will hopefully be used by hundreds or thousands of customers in a wide variety of ways and contexts takes at least TEN times longer and far more effort than developing a basic software program or solution for a private user. This where all that nasty, time-consuming, and highly-detailed work called implementation, configuration and customization comes in which – by the way – rarely scales.

Are the Savings, Flexibility and New Functionality Worth the Risks to My Business?

Drivers of electric cars suffer from "range" anxiety. They worry about whether their current charge will last long enough to get home or to the next charging station. Thoughtful and attentive SaaS users should suffer constantly from "change" anxiety for two reasons. First, another portion of the half-a-loaf problem is that, as a SaaS customer (whether you realize it or not), you only get effective control over your part of the total package. This makes for the serious likelihood of some very nasty surprises whenever the main operating system in the cloud is changed, updated or otherwise revised – with or without ample notice to you and rarely with testing sufficient to confirm that the new versions will work with your install. Think of the overall installation as having two parts (theirs and yours) and ANY time that the two parts get out of sync, you're basically screwed.

Ultimately, I feel that the real problem is a structural one – the vendors are worried about enhancing and improving their main set of offerings and solutions and you're praying (because you've spent a small fortune configuring and customizing your end of their system so that it works with and for your business) that whatever changes they make won't damage or disrupt your operations. I hope that you don't think for a minute that there are ANY SaaS vendors out there who test their new updates and revisions against every customer's installation and usage BEFORE they release the new versions. That would be far too difficult and time-consuming as well as impossibly costly to staff and support.

And it gets worse. No small start-up can realistically afford (whether they admit it to you or not) to build and be running a completely separate development environment alongside their production systems. That's just not the way the world or the money works in the start-up universe. And, as a result, they release their changes into the production environment and – as noted above – they do their testing on you and your business in real time. This is the fundamental risk of a cloud-based solution. One size and one version or system will never work for any serious number of customers and frankly the attitude in the SaaS world isn't to make the system work for the customers. Once these businesses have any real traction and installed bases, their attitude is that you need to decide whether their system will work for you and – if it doesn't – they respectfully suggest that you change your business processes until it does.

One Last Thing to Think About

And remember one final thing – in addition to determining whether the vendor's sales people are telling you the truth and whether the references they provide are legitimate and satisfied users (or just fellow victims looking for company) - you have to weigh and consider the agendas and the motivations of the people <u>inside your company</u> as well. In every case I have seen (or suffered through myself), there are well-intentioned and sincere people on both sides of the decision with decent reasons to support their arguments and then there is usually another collection of people who are scared to make any decision that they might be blamed for; afraid to rock the boat or change things; committed to prior solutions that they endorsed or recommended; protecting their own job, people, turf or fiefdoms; and/or just too lazy to want to do the work that it takes to do one of these migrations well. They are rarely incented to give you the straight scoop.

Information (along with hard questions and sharp edges) has a way of getting smoothed out and softened as it wends its way upward in your organization on its way to your desk. That's just another fact of life – regardless of how big or little your headcount is. Just be sure you have all the facts before you make your move.

SOMETIMES GOOD ENOUGH IS GOOD ENOUGH

I spent some time recently with a very talented and thoughtful team of young entrepreneurs from Pathful (www.pathful.com) who were developing some new analytical tools to help non-technical website owners determine which parts of their websites were effective for them (driving engagement, conversion and ultimately sales) and which other parts either weren't as successful or, worse yet, were actually damaging to their business because they aggravated, frustrated or confused visitors and ultimately turned them off.

This is a bigger problem and a much bigger deal today for business owners than you might imagine (and, most likely, it's a problem for you as well) because – while everyone tells us (regardless of our size or type of business) that we need a website – no one (including the companies who build and host the websites) ever tells us (the site owners) with any precision or detail whether the website is really "working" for us and/or whether it's worth the time and investment which we've made (and continue to make) in it. Try it yourself. If you call up your website developer, provider or host today and ask how your site is doing, at best, you'll get some "up-time" data and maybe some traffic information, but nothing that really deals with the real metrics and ROI of the website.

As I learned more about this new business, one very appealing aspect of their SAAS-based service was how highly automated the back-end processing and reporting systems were going to be and how – as a result – they could cost-effectively offer some basic versions of their products, services and reports at prices which would be reasonably affordable and which would appeal to early-stage businesses (as well as many Mom & Pop businesses) all of which they clearly understood wouldn't and couldn't afford or justify the costs of licensing and implementing some of the higher-end and much more expensive analytics packages which have been in the market for a while. Another of the best aspects of their new offerings was how quick and "easy" they said it would for a business to deploy their software and start getting valuable feedback. They simply had to "add a couple of lines of *Java* script" to their site and they were ready to roll. Just like implementing some of *Google*'s basic tools.

And that's where I started to get worried that they were about to become victims of their own narrow environment and technical expertise. Because when you're sitting in a start-up incubator or a shared tech workspace killing it with your team and you're all surrounded by dozens (or even hundreds) of other smart, young techies who eat *Java* script for breakfast, it's a lot like living in an echo chamber lined with mirrors.

Everyone hears what they want and perhaps even what they need to hear in order to keep going, but - by and large - they simply have very little idea of how life actually works outside their bubble in the real (very pedestrian and non-technical) world. Especially if one of your prime market target sectors are young and small businesses. Telling a small business owner that all he needs to do is to "add a little code" to his website is a lot like handing him a pen knife and telling him that it's cheaper and easier to just do his own root canal. And he doesn't even need to make an appointment.

And there's a second, equally problematic, aspect of this type of situation which I call the "curse of creeping functionality". It's driven by talent and enthusiasm and the best of intentions, but it can really hurt a start-up by resulting in product offerings that are too complex and ambitious and way too over-engineered and technical for the larger market. They may suit and please the earliest adopters, but they're gonna freak out the crowd. The fact is that the "boys in the back room" just want to keep on building great code and adding more and more to the company's products, but here's the nasty news: new products and services have to satisfy the immediate needs of prospective customers and current users and not the egos or desires of the company's managers and engineers.

For so many companies today that are tech-based, this is a really difficult growth phase to navigate and it can easily lead to hurt feelings, abrupt departures of key employees and plenty of other problems including a lot of passive-aggressive behavior and foot-dragging from the geeks. But if you're the CEO and you're building the right kind of business, then you've also got to be the customers' and users' advocate; rein in the troops; and make sure that your products meet the market's needs and not the other way around.

Existing users are incrementalists – they are generally at least willing to try system enhancements and updates as long as these are not disruptive of their ongoing activities. New prospects, on the other hand, are always looking for an easy on-ramp and a simple way to start. They don't want to read a book, take a training course, or spend a week getting up to speed – they just want to get started. For the vast majority of customers, too many bells and whistles (products that "can do whatever you want") are not attractive enticements or incentives; they're perceived headaches and anticipated heartburn in the making. Prospects and new customers don't want tools that can do "anything" – that's not a meaningful or useful concept for them – in fact, it's most often off-putting and too vague to help convince them of anything. Basically, they want solutions to serious, finite and obvious needs that they have to solve pressing problems which are important to them. Now I will admit that they may not even know that they have some of these problems until they're "sold" on the need for a solution, but I can also promise you that they want a solution in a box and not a set of D.I.Y. instructions telling them how to build the scaffolding and infrastructure that they'll need to solve their problems.

Now, don't get me wrong. For many companies with the right staff and support, adding a powerful, effective and inexpensive tool like this to their website would be a no-brainer and a very smart thing to do. I understand that not everything can be natural, easy, user-friendly and taste like chocolate. But for the millions of little guys all over the country who really need and could benefit from this kind of objective, third-party review of the value and effectiveness of their sites, identifying the problem for them, but then offering them only a partial solution which they can't take advantage of or implement themselves is a waste of everyone's time and effort.

And yet, if you step back and really look at what the customer's problem is that you are trying to solve (what's the "job" that needs to get done) rather than getting locked into a perspective of focusing on all the great things your new service and software can do and create, it's actually pretty easy to figure out a better answer and a much better offering. In this particular case, the problem is very clear: if the customer is paralyzed or afraid or incapable of adding the couple of lines of simple code to his website, you've got to figure out how to add it remotely (or through a channel partner like BrightTag   www.brighttag.com) for him. Once it's there, everything else is easy. I'm thinking something along the lines of a next-generation, no-brainer *InstallShield* kind of download that the customer just emails to the host of his site although an interesting question is whether those gatekeepers are gonna be happy to help or pains in the ass to get around.

Basically, you've got to solve the WHOLE problem for these little guys and, once you figure out how to do that, you discover that there's a huge, readily scalable market sitting right in front of you. And as long as you entirely solve at least part of the problem, it's not critical at the outset that your solution does everything, addresses all the issues, provides every form of report, etc. That can all come later – but only if you can get a foot or two in the door and get started. This is really what disruptive innovation is all about – start small, listen aggressively, iterate and then scale.

And the best part of this approach is that, once you can eliminate the major barrier to acceptance (the *Java* script addition to the website in this case) and get yourself onboard, you discover that the bar for substantial success is embarrassingly low. Sometimes simple is more than sufficient for a large segment of the market. Good enough in this case can be more than good enough. You can make this low-end, high-volume, automated version of your product or service easier, simpler, and less robust, etc. because these companies aren't power users or sophisticated buyers; they're customers who would be grateful for any help in this area. And the more hand-holding, explaining, and straightforward analysis that you can do for them, even at the most basic level, the more appreciative and satisfied they will be.

DON'T BUILD YOUR BIZ ON A PINNACLE

I t used to be a sign of disrespect and condemnation to say that someone had their head in the clouds. They were foolish dreamers or cock-eyed optimists - certainly not the kind of down-to-earth folks firmly grounded in reality that anyone with any brains would want to bet on and/or invest in. Thoreau wrote about people building castles in the air (which he said was where they should be), but then he cautioned that the next steps needed to be putting solid foundations under them.

Right now, you can't go anywhere without hearing or seeing another pitch for SaaS and enduring multiple arguments for putting your products and services in the cloud. I wrote about SaaS not too long ago myself although my view – then as now – was a pretty contrary one. (See: Why SaaS is More Dangerous than It Looks. http://www.inc.com/howard-tullman/why-saas-is-more-dangerous-than-it-looks.html). As it happens, being in the cloud today is supposed to be way cool. Everyone will tell you that it's definitely the place for your business to be. But I'd say "maybe". Because I think it depends entirely on what kind of business you're planning to build and whether you've built the right foundation for moving forward.

This is because sometimes - especially in the world of technology - you learn that the more things seem to change, the more they stay the same and you eventually realize that they're no different than they've always been. I don't want to rain on anyone's parade, but the cloud's no more a panacea and the answer to all things than any of the other wondrous tools and technologies that came before it. The cloud can kick-start you or kill you if you're not careful. And sadly, if your head's stuck up there in the haze and you think the cloud's gonna solve everything for you and your business, you're likely to be just as mistaken and wrong-headed today as you would have been years ago which was – by the way - long before we all discovered the supposedly silver linings inside all those newly-accessible and suddenly transparent clouds.

If your business plan and model are appropriate, the cloud could be a big help, but if your model makes no sense, nothing including the cloud will make much of a difference. Because when you really look closely, you discover that the cloud's not magic or another Oz – it's just a virtual place in cyberspace - an environment to operate in - and for your startup to be successful anywhere - in the ether or down on Earth - you've still got to build a business that's well-grounded and smart. There's no question that the cloud's cheap and easy in many ways, but there are plenty of things that you just shouldn't ever do for your business and trying to do them cheaply is much worse than not doing them at all. So it pays to do your homework before you head into the ozone. And, in particular, that's why, when you're thinking about the cloud and your business model, it's so important to pay attention to exactly what you're trying to build.

Pinnacles are a Problem

Pinnacles are generally very tall and relatively thin. They're a very precarious foundation for a business because they don't provide a broad base of user engagement or commitment or support and they really limit your ability to connect to your customers and, more importantly, to react to and/or cushion the impact of adverse developments. The cloud encourages us to chase the world and boil the ocean from Day One because those opportunities are theoretically there for the taking. But, if you fall for the long thin line (essentially the polar opposite of the long tail), you find that you're stretched way out (a mile high and an inch wide) and that a relatively modest upset, piece of bad news, or other disturbance can really knock your whole enterprise off course because your real connection to so many of your remote and very distant customers is so tenuous. To build a smart business, you never want to be spread too widely or have too thin a connection to your users and this is how I see a number of businesses today.

You want to be focused, but not single-threaded – you want to be straight, but not narrow – and you always want to have a couple of ways out of the tight spots. And it's pretty easy to drink your own Kool-Aid if you're not careful. For example, if you're disrupting and revolutionizing an industry where the standards of response time and performance were historically measured in days or weeks, you don't have to introduce your new solution and your initial metrics in terms of minutes or hours of turn-around time. Give yourself a break and some breathing room. It's always easier to improve than to walk the customers back from some insane, unscalable and hyper-costly benchmark that you simply made up.

This is an area where too much information – being too data-driven – can actually limit your opportunities and your upside while increasing your vulnerability because you can fall in love with the measurements and lose sight of the critical relationships and your real business objectives. Take measuring turn-around or response times (as noted above) or tracking geographic penetration as examples.

Measurement is a relativist thing and when we are constantly measuring our results against purely pre-defined goals and objectives, it's too easy to develop a case of tunnel vision. As the data tell us that we are drawing ever nearer to the goal ("our uptime is great and our response time is terrific") and we convince ourselves that we're getting better and better ("we have customers in 50 countries"), we lose sight of the fact that (a) these may be easy things to measure, but they aren't necessarily the important things to focus on or optimize for the long run; (b) too much of a good thing probably isn't a good thing if it's too soon to manage it; and (c) there may be much larger and broader opportunities over the horizon and outside of our immediate zones of interest and – while we're feeling so good about our near-term progress – someone else is out there getting ready to steal the main prize out from under us.

Because the cloud can so readily and inexpensively connect us to many or just a few users everywhere and because it enables degrees of unimaginable and constant connectivity, it is very seductive and it's very easy to run down these rabbit holes and lose your way. You can quickly end up over-extended, under-manned and unable to meet the commitments you've made to your users and customers. It's pretty lonely and uncomfortable sitting on top of that pinnacle wondering what went wrong. But at least it's not crowded.

NOTHING'S MORE POWERFUL
THAN A PLATFORM

People casually talk about "the cloud" as a platform, but it's not. It's just an alternative method of data conveyance. Most simply stated, it's a part of the pipe that gets you to and from whatever platform (think resource repository) you're looking for where you can access, connect to, interact with, and/or extract whatever you need. The cloud has solved the classic distribution dilemma which has dogged millions of young businesses since the beginning of time. How do I get my product or service offering out there to the masses? Solving that riddle is far more possible today through multiple channels – especially the app stores – than ever before.

In the old days, the name of the game used to be all about location. But in today's hyper-mobile world of constant connectivity, location is essentially immaterial (work itself is also no longer place-based) and effective distribution is all that matters. The cloud (basically for free to the end user) makes access ubiquitous and response time close to instantaneous. This is compelling and tremendously helpful (as well as cost-effective), but the real value and the ultimate power still resides with the parties who control the contents and the underlying delivery platform itself – not in the pipes. We see tiny, but very clear examples of the relative power of the players every time some cable company tries to extort additional carriage fees from content providers. All these games eventually end up in the same way – the guys with the goods get the gold – and the pipe guys are sent packing and back to the woodshed.

But when I talk about platforms, I'm not talking about the basic technology platforms (iOS6, Jelly Bean or Windows 8) that run our devices; I'm talking about the data, content and transaction platforms (or you might think of them as bi-lateral networks) which are sitting on top of these enabling technologies and which connect us with the data we desire, cool content of every kind, necessary products and services or simply other people.

And by the way, if you're wondering why there are only 3 mobile platforms (actually 2 ½ to be honest); that will tell you something important in itself about the power of platforms. Platforms are central to the "winner-take-all" realities of the world of technology and they help to create the inevitable concentration in these markets where one or two winners outdistance the field and then enjoy disproportionate and substantial profits for as long a time as their dominance persists. And these windfall and excess profits – if aggressively deployed – can further accelerate the ability of the leaders to pull away from the pack in many different ways. Excess cash can be applied to securing priority positions and placements in critical channels, crowding the channels themselves and closing out available ad inventory or other exposure available for competitors, predatory pricing, etc.

The fact is that, in markets fundamentally driven and dominated by (a) two or three central platforms, (b) mission-critical technologies, (c) ubiquitous operating systems; (d) enabling networks; or (e) products with very little, possibly zero, marginal production and distribution costs; over some reasonably short period of time, there will consistently emerge a clear and obvious winner, a strong number two and then a bunch of midgets and also-rans. There's just not enough volume or oxygen in these intensely competitive markets to support a half dozen winners. All of the structural considerations inherent in the ways we (as customers and consumers) elect to narrow and concentrate our choices rather than broadening the scope of our inquiries and our horizons also help to reinforce and precisely dictate the result we see over and over again in these case. Whether it's time constraints, an interest in efficiency, pure ignorance, sheer laziness or just basic human nature, we all tend to pick (and stick with) our familiar favorites.

There are a number of other contributing factors to this recurring outcome which are less personal – demonstrated economies of scale, market-dictated centralization and standardization requirements, and, of course, the power of Metcalfe's Law which first described and defined the exponential growth characteristics of networks and how that growth rapidly increased the network's power, resilience and value. The more power and connections a business had to and with its users, the more powerful and profitable it would become.

Metcalfe's law with certain subsequent refinements and embellishments stated that the value of any network (originally consisting of connected and bilaterally communicating inanimate devices, but these days counting nodes of any kind including people and/or users) was proportional to the square of the number of connections. If anything, in today's world of constant connectivity where every one of us is tethered to one or more devices at all times, the predictive power and nearly universal application of Metcalfe is even more relevant.

So your mission is pretty clear. If you want to find the prime position for your business to capture value from whatever back-and-forth activity is going on in your industry; you're going to want to identify the convergence points within the market – through which virtually all of the traffic and commerce needs to pass – and that's where your business needs to be. If you can locate the hub (not the spokes) and get yourself on the gatekeeper gravy train;

you will learn very quickly just how powerful a position this can be. Being paid even a little something every time anything moves over a network adds up to a whole lot of everything in pretty short order.

And here's the deal: you don't have to be some Colossus astride the harbor to pull this off. Smart little guys can often construct effective horizontal platforms more quickly and economically than the big vertical (and siloed) players who dominate many (mainly oligopolistic) markets. You just need to understand the basic building blocks and the dynamics of what makes a particular platform prevail. And you need to plan to be a platform from Day One. Believe me, it's not something you stumble into.

So what do you need to know and be thinking about in terms of creating a persistent and winning platform as you try to build and properly position your own business?

(1) Do Something for the Market that the Major Players Can't Do Collectively or for Themselves

There are any number of industries where the major players are prevented by law or regulations from collaborative or cooperative efforts (very often these laws specifically target pricing issues) which are almost automatically regarded by the authorities and regulators not as helpful, but as predatory, exclusionary and anti-competitive. This makes it very difficult to structure and organize some market solutions that might ultimately be very beneficial and cost-effective for the consumer and which – at least arguably - ought to be of equal interest and concern to the same regulators. At the same time, these situations create great opportunities and openings for little guys to come out of nowhere and create sustainable new solutions.

So, in the case of the book publishers and Apple (albeit at Amazon's urging), the government attorneys have sued, fined and/or settled with almost all of the players for "conspiring to fix book prices". But, in the streaming music space, (where the music moguls seem to have finally learned a few lessons from the Napster debacle), we have Spotify and Shazam and others providing new services to consumers. And guess what? By creating industry-wide platforms for music delivery, these aggressive little startup companies not only blew the big guys away, but – even better yet – invited them in as investors. At last count, Spotify investors included: Sony BMG at 5.8 percent, Universal Music at 4.8 percent, Warner Music at 3.8 percent and EMI at 1. 9 percent. Also Merlin holds a small stake. The story is pretty much the same with Shazam where Sony, Universal (Vivendi) and Warner (Access Industries) each invested the exact same amount of $3 million. Could the message they are sending be any clearer? A very convenient and "legal" way for the very same guys who couldn't do it themselves to do it together thru smart startups building next-gen platforms.

(2) Create Criteria or Objective Benchmarks that Become the De Facto Industry Standards

A second path to becoming an industry platform deals with a different issue that again is common in many industries and presents new opportunities in all of them. In markets dominated by a few majors, a common problem in organizing and improving the efficiency of the market and creating better visibility (and "apples-to-apples" price comparison capability) for consumer is the lack of common and consistent nomenclature and the fact that each of the players has adopted and is psychologically "stuck" with their own numbering, identifying and classifying systems for their products even though the products offered by multiple players are functionally and often physically identical.

There are a lot of reasons for this – companies that believe that their branding and reputation will permit them to charge the consumer more for a product that is basically a commodity come to mind as the type of player which will resist market standardization. But they are basically losers (or will shortly be) in the new world of transparency where even the laziest consumer willing to do the minimal amount of research can access almost perfect pricing data in a flash. Another reason for the resistance to change and improved market organization and efficiency is simply company pride of authorship and the "not invented here" syndrome. This is "how we do it" and we always will do it this way – flash – until the market tells them otherwise by moving quickly away from them. And a final complication is simple overkill. Many companies for reasons ranging from tradition to the requirements of antiquated legacy accounting and control systems have way too much information associated with every product in their inventory and accounting systems. This does nothing good for anyone and, in fact, creates additional impediments to the company's speed, competitive responses to changed market conditions, etc.

Not surprisingly, the solutions which are changing markets like these are again being created by startups who are unhampered by all the historical and traditional concerns (as well as the ego issues) that make it hard to innovate and improve the old ways of doing things in the big businesses that dominate these industries.

And, in addition to being free of the constraints of the past, these startups bring a fresh approach which can best be described by three critical words: "Good Enough Is". They aren't trying to write the Magna Carta for product classification or the Geneva Convention (worthless as that may be in its own right) for generating inventory lists; they are just interested in building a simple new solution that spans horizontally across the many market players and focuses only on the common and critical components and characteristics that matter to the market when specifications and purchase decisions are being made. Nothing needs to be perfect – nothing needs to be the "be-all and the end-all" – the solution that gets you started just needs to work and be good enough to get the job done. Things can and will always get better, but they won't ever happen if you don't get something started in the first place.

Need a simple example? Think about eBay way back when. No real product specifications. No serial numbers and other details. Not even photos in many cases at the beginning. But it became a powerful trading platform in very short order because it was a sufficient system to get the required job done. While customer expectations are definitely progressive over time; they're pretty primitive and modest at the outset of a new experience.

(3) <u>Offer the End Users/Customers Independent and Consistent Evaluation Documentation</u>

A third type of platform is one which creates a resource for buyers and sellers to access accurate, independent, and consistent documentation about the location, availability and costs of various products (often used or refurbished) which is not often available from the sellers or manufacturers of new equipment. In theory, the best type of platform for this particular need would be an active marketplace, but because it is often difficult and time-consuming to assemble a critical mass of buyers and sellers at the outset and sufficient transaction volume as well – the marketplace is a nice and desirable tool for generating the pricing and supply/demand data about various products – but it's not necessarily the only solution in the short term.

Better and more accurate information is always preferable, but in some cases, any information that helps the parties make smart and more informed choices is better than nothing. When I started CCC Information Services in 1980, the goal was exactly this – to provide in digital formats better, more accurate, and more timely information about used car prices for insurance adjusters and ultimately for consumers to use in settling insurance loss claims. 35 years later, the same basic platform that I built back then is still in use and CCC is still the industry leader in the insurance vehicle valuation space.

What's so great about working with innovative startups every day at 1871 is that I get to see new and exciting game-changing examples of businesses addressing some of the same issues I dealt with decades before, but applying them to new markets and opportunities. One case in point is MarkITx (an early 1871 company) which is building a platform to permit Fortune 1000 companies to efficiently value and then buy or sell the billions of dollars of used IT equipment that they have to update and dispose of every year.

Right now, in 90% of the cases, my impression is that the only important consideration for these companies is getting rid of the old stuff (someway, somehow) in order to quickly make room for the new stuff. The fact that they regard it as "junk" and that they have foolishly written the equipment down far too quickly on their books results in them leaving tens of millions of dollars on the floor of the shipping dock while some junk dealer drags the old stuff away.

A system like the one MarkITx is already putting in place for major firms with enormous dated equipment inventories that simply and accurately not only shows them the actual residual value of the pieces that they were about to pitch, but then also painlessly enables them to sell those items for cash on the barrel head has been a long time coming. But it's here now. And, just as you would expect, once you've got your shop set up on this kind of an automated system with a disposal schedule, etc. and you can just look forward to the "found money" rolling back into your coffers on a regular basis, you don't even think about doing something else or going elsewhere.

(4) Invest Your Resources in Infrastructure Individual Market Players Couldn't Justify or Afford to Create for Themselves

Another of the opportunity spaces for platforms are in markets not dominated by a few big guys, but consisting instead of a million little guys – none of whom are in a position to make the commitment or the capital investments (as well as absorbing the people costs) of funding the costs involved in launching, marketing and operating a central organizing platform for their industry or marketplace. As I said above, platforms don't happen accidentally and getting the word out about a centralized and ubiquitous utility platform is very tough and very expensive.

I'm somewhat surprised that even sophisticated business journalists often don't really get what's going on in these spaces. One writer whose opinions I generally respect commented on Uber and said he wasn't even sure that Uber was a technology company. He acknowledged that they used smartphones, but so, he said, did every other business these days including taxi companies. Frankly, he just didn't understand that it wasn't about the phone you used, it was all about the classic Ghostbusters question. Who ya gonna call? That's the name of the platform game. Sure everyone in the city could just call some random cab company on their phone from wherever they happened to be and hope for the best, but that's not a solution that anyone with any smarts thinks is a winner.

To solve this riddle, you've got to be top of mind with the consumer; have immediately responsive city-wide coverage; have a critical mass of participating drivers – 24/7; build a system to instantly connect them all thru a single distributed platform; and then have lots of cash and staying power and hope for the best.

Anyone who thinks this isn't a technology business won't know a Tesla from a Model T.

So, at the end of the day, one thing is absolutely clear. It will be the companies driving and controlling the centralized and coordinated connections we need through the hubs, the networks, and the other emergent channels which will be the ones which can extract market-driven premiums from the communications, transactions and commerce moving through them. These gatekeepers (many of them startups who built the critical platforms) will keep a very fair share of the gold. Nothing primes a platform.

HOW RIDESCOUT GOT IT RIGHT

Way back when, in April of 2013, Scott Case and I participated in a rapid pitch program called Enrich Your Pitch at the INC. GROWCO conference in New Orleans. The competition featured all veteran-owned and operated businesses as the presenting companies. It was an impressive group and I was especially taken with an eager guy named Joseph Kopser who was pitching his relatively new business, Ridescout. At the time, I didn't realize quite how new it was.

Joe didn't win the grand prize, but he says that the press and the exposure from the event were worth their weight in gold from investors and helped him keep afloat and raise crucial funds at a very precarious time. He also told me - much more recently - that - at the time of his GROWCO pitch - he barely had a beta version of his idea and he was having an impossible time hanging on to users. In any event, we hit it off in the Big Easy and have been in regular touch ever since.

Now flash forward about a year or so, and Joe picks a luncheon at 1871 in Chicago as the place to launch Ridescout in the Midwest. The business literally exploded after that event into another 66 cities in a matter of weeks. It was a spectacular rollout and Joe has been running around the country ever since with 69 total active markets and several hundred ride providers. I thought I knew exactly what his game plan was – in fact – I wrote about the basic components of the strategy in two recent INC. columns about the power of platforms which are described below, but I still wanted to hear it from the horse's mouth.

Luckily for us, Joe still finds time to swing by his 1871 Chicago office on a regular basis and, most recently, in addition to promoting Ridescout, he's become a vocal and very active supporter of a new initiative that we have launched at 1871 called The Bunker which is an incubator and support program for veteran-owned businesses with a particular focus on technology. The Bunker is led by Todd Connor who is a Navy man and it launched formally a few weeks ago as part of the 1871 2.0 expansion program. We were honored to host the event which was attended by over 300 interested supporters, members, investors and vets as well as by U.S. Senator Dick Durbin, the senior senator from Illinois. And, of course, Joe was there at the Bunker launch as well because giving back and helping out is also a big part of who he is and what he wants to do with his life.

And then – just a couple of weeks later – came the big announcement that Daimler, one of the world's largest car manufacturer, had acquired Ridescout and entered the ride-sharing business. Quite another impressive step up for a startup that was scrambling to survive a little more than a year ago, but that's how it happens if you're in the right place with the right team and the right idea at the right time. And, of course, it never happens by accident.

So I sat down recently with Joe to ask him exactly what the secrets were to that drove the rapid national expansion and brought about all the good things that followed. And, in a word, he said that he basically built a "platform" which, of course, was music to my ears and exactly what I had assumed. And it's amazing how closely his description on the critical building blocks mirrored my recent INC. pieces.

What the Power of the Platform Means for Your Company covered parts 1 and 2 of the strategy: (a) do what the big guys can't do for themselves or won't do by working together; and (b) create de <u>facto</u> industry standards that organize otherwise unstructured data and markets.

Joe figured out early on that each of the alternative transportation providers was operating in a silo and the last thing that any of them cared about or was focused on was cooperating on sharing route and cost data - even if such a combination was clearly desired and highly valuable and beneficial for the end user. Basically, Ridescout built the bridge between these islands and created a comprehensive platform that served the consumer's needs.

Even more importantly, Joe understood that each vendor had their own language, terminology, interfaces, etc. and that the absolutely last thing any consumer needed were more individual apps on their phones which didn't talk to each other and which couldn't even be effectively compared with one another without investing an inordinate amount of time and energy.

The need for a one-stop shopping experience and an integrated solution was clear, but no one was really in a position to get the job done. Needless to say, the first mover would have a major shot at organizing the entire space, setting the industry standards, and becoming the market leader. Ridescout rode to the rescue.

The Primacy of the Platform dealt with the third major consideration: invest your energy and resources in building infrastructure that the individual players in a given market can't afford to do by themselves.

So the need was clear and there was a major opportunity, but Joe also needed to assemble the technical team that could get the job done quickly and in a fashion that was immediately scalable. He needed to build a platform and an overall solution that accomplished 4 things:

1. It was absolutely critical to figure out how to translate, aggregate and normalize the data which needed to be "grabbed" from sites, suppliers and vendors from all over the country into a consistent set of formats. Building the ingest tools and the translation programs were major time and dollar investments.

2. It was equally important to build a single interface for all sharing by vertical – in other words – all bike shares needed to ultimately look the same thru Ridescout regardless of the city you were in – and the same was true for all car shares, transit and rides for hire. No one else was stepping up to fund the development of a single standard and one which also needed to somehow account for the outliers in certain areas whose particular approaches needed to be melded into the overall system.

3. The system and the backend had to be scalable and robust enough on Day One to accommodate the flood of data (and hopefully users) as well as demand from newly interested participating vendor and partners – once they woke up – on a national basis and the process needed to be as automated as possible.

4. The overall solution set needed to be extensible and always backwardly compatible because the only way to make sure that Ridesout maintained its leadership position was to constantly be raising the bar by adding features and functionality that responded to the input, suggestions, complaints and increasing demands and expectations of all the participants including the various governmental bodies in each geographic location. As it happened, the fact that Ridescout took a very conciliatory and collaborative

approach to the city managers and regulatory bodies as they moved from market to market turned out to create a very substantial barrier for other potential new entrants.

Ultimately, time will tell, but Joe's off on an exciting and exploding ride and nothing beats a well thought-out and a well-built platform as long as you keep raising the bar.

YOU ARE WHAT YOU ARE INTERESTED IN

When Facebook bought Karma (one of the leading gift sites) at the end of 2012, it was pretty clear that we were going to see a second iteration of Facebook Gifts - especially as the holiday shopping season started to heat up. Socially-informed commerce in various forms and shapes has been around for quite a while, but we're at another major inflection point now because of the impact of hyper-personalization and the far more precise and cost-effective targeting which is now available.

Keep in mind that it's a long-established principle that, if you give a consumer too many choices, they are far more likely to buy nothing than if you give them a limited and more relevant decision set. New young companies like Chicago-based Local Offer Network are jumping into this particular space as well with tools that deliver the "exactly right" offers to consumers visiting a site even the first time that the visitor appears. I call this "smart reach" and Facebook will be all over it – especially with Facebook Exchange.

Given the tools and resources that Facebook increasingly has at its disposal, they can now make the gift selection and giving process far more successful for the donor and also make the recipient far more likely to be happy with the gift. Remember that the excellence of a gift lies in its appropriateness, not simply in its value. And there are other important ancillary benefits as well. One of the reasons people get divorced is that they run out of gift ideas. Ergo – better gifts – less divorces.

So there's no question that this latest foray into "f-commerce" is going to be a big focus for the Facebook team along with a couple of other "interest graph-driven" initiatives like Facebook "Collections" which is their initial salvo in response to the explosive growth of Pinterest. If you want to get some idea of how interesting and accurate gift giving becomes when it's informed by detailed data about the interests and preferences and buying history of the friends and peers for whom you're trying to select a present, take a look at shopycat.com which is actually a product created by Wal-Mart Labs - but very cool nonetheless.

If you are more of a metrics person, here are some numbers to keep in mind – when a "friend" refers and/or recommends that someone they know take an action on the web – the impact (as compared to a simple ad solicitation) is major: recipients are 15% more likely to download something; 8% more likely to buy something; and – most importantly – when they do buy, the average order size is 22% larger. That's a lotta lift.

What's less obvious about the new gift-giving initiatives (the Lightbank/Groupon gang also invested in Boomerang in 2012 which is another gift site) is that, from Facebook's perspective, the dollars generated from gift purchases may be nowhere near as valuable in the long run to their enterprise as the purchase decision data which will be made available through these transactions as well as the implicit and explicit "connections" which each and every gift transaction will establish between their members. You can just imagine the opportunities for follow-on sales and service and the cross-marketing possibilities that each gift will create.

As I like to say, "personal data is the oil of the digital age" and Facebook increasingly owns the primary pump. And because birds of a feather flock together, other analytical tools will help correlate purchases with the buyer's presence in defined communities and other likely behavioral groups. Data, data and more data with virtually no acquisition cost and high degrees of precision and accuracy.

So the real "news" about Facebook Gifts is that we're continuing to see more and more indications of the next major seismic shift from the relatively simple social graph to the deeper interest graph. Because we (and Facebook in particular) have pretty much cracked the code on personal data and demographics (empowered in real-time by high-velocity computing), the next hurdle is pretty clear: "tell me what you're interested in and what you pay attention to and I will tell you who you are". And basically, if you're not where your targets and customers are and a relevant part of their world, you're nowhere. This is really where both Instagram, Aviary and Pinterest loom large.

As we see better and better tools to interpret and identify (and categorize) visual materials (photos and other images with videos to follow in the near future), we will see more and more emphasis on and influence of the players who are successfully aggregating these huge treasure troves of visual information. After all, a picture's worth about a million words these days if it's the right picture.

And speaking about the future and gifts reminds me that the future isn't a gift, it's an achievement that we work for and earn every day. Hard work is what makes our dreams come true.

But Facebook really is like a powerful steamroller and it rarely stops changing the rules of the game - and thereby - the world that we all live in today. The addition of Facebook Graph Search is really another major brick in the wall. But it's really a double-edged sword that will take some serious getting used to.

I've been worried for a while about the filter bubble and how narrow the search process was becoming as it increasingly morphed from a window on new worlds to a mirror reflecting back to us basically what we and our friends already know. Our peers are important, but how would you learn anything new if search was simply an endless loop?

I was also concerned about the death of serendipitous discovery which is the sheer joy we feel at a bookstore (remember those?) or a flea market (remember those?) when we come across something new and amazing and totally unexpected and it just makes our day. You didn't even know you were looking for something, but you loved it when you found it. And, of course, in search terms, you could never have constructed a query to find something you weren't seeking.

That's why I'm excited about Graph Search and why it will actually enable and enhance a lot of businesses (besides Facebook's) which could include yours once you understand some of the basics beneath the buzz.

First and foremost, GS is a return to the earliest days and, in fact, to the origin of Facebook. Think about it (even if you've only seen the movie) – it was about finding pictures of the hottest women on campus. And, clearly, it wasn't about women you knew (search); it was about women you wanted (desperately) to know (discovery).

GS takes the blinders and the filters off of the painstaking process of conscious search (does anyone really want to check out all of your friends' profiles one at a time?) and opens up a huge amount of additional social and personal and interest material that was always there, but which is now readily accessible. Broad content queries constrained by the limiters and filters of your friends is an elegant way to get right to the heart of the interest graph.

Two simple examples – how much better would a *Groupon* deal do if in 10 seconds I could ask Facebook which of my friends were already participating in the deal? Or have *Ticketmaster*'s concert seating charts (enabled by Facebook integration) show me which of my friends already have tickets to the show and where they are sitting?

So, as you start to think about how to position your business and your product and service offerings in new ways to make them discoverable and sharable thru the new power of Graph Search, keep in mind the following three aspects of GS:

(1) <u>Aggregation</u>

GS does the heavy lifting for you and assembles the data and results of your friends' likes, preferences and interests across whatever cuts and selections you care to make and permits you to interactively build on your questions and broaden or narrow them on the fly. Single friends with MBAs who are living in San Francisco and working in the entertainment business? You got it in a flash.

(2) <u>Filters</u>

Instead of limiting your queries or your results in the background in ways that were never really clear, filters now take on a new ability to help you frame your selections, criteria and choices in ways that avoid overwhelming and unwieldy results and permit you to dictate limits of scope, time, location, images, etc. Friends who loved *Inglourious Basterds* and are actually up for going to see *Django* with me? Try that on Google.

(3) <u>Engagement</u>

For now, and this may change, assets like photos are "valued" and ranked and displayed in engagement order which – in Facebook terms – means that the more likes and comments a particular photo has, the more likely it will be to be surfaced. The reason I think that this criteria is in flux is that it's highly likely that the volume of activity around a photo may be exactly why it's the least likely photo that the person shown in the photo wants circulated.

We're headed into the next big burst of Facebook-enabled commerce (f-commerce) and increasingly millions of customers are going to be living within this Facebook economy and nowhere else. If you doubt that, just check out how many times the Facebook team during the launch events repeated the idea that "you never have to leave Facebook" to do anything that you want to do.

Each of these components of the new GS engine will change many of the ground rules for how (and whether) new and small businesses will be able to make themselves heard and get their messages out to their prospective customers in the clutter and the crowd. It's not going to be easier, but it will definitely be more interesting.

Here's one last word of advice. One of the great internal mantras of Facebook regarding the creation of all social web content is: what will make them care? and what will make them share? As you bring your products and services to market, keep these two questions top of mind.

GOOGLE'S GROWING APP GAP

T wo weeks ago was the 25th anniversary of the World Wide Web. Even for those of us who were there at the very beginning, it's hard to remember a time before the Internet. But the sad truth is that the Web, as we once knew it, is disappearing right before our eyes. Does anyone type "www" as part of an URL anymore? Does anyone type a URL anymore or really want to type anything? I think not.

We'd rather swipe a screen or press a button on our phone or, better yet, just tell our phone what it is that we need. In fact, whether we like to admit it or not, we'd actually much prefer for our devices to "know" what we need before we ask based on our preferences, interests, location, prior behaviors and profiles. Then, without having to ask, we'd just have the answers handy and readily available when, where and whenever we need them. I call this modality "MOCIAL" – the merger of mobile and social – which is driven and enabled by constant connectivity, high-velocity computing, and by the massive stores of data about all of us which are now accessible to virtually anyone at little or no cost. These new capabilities and tools set standards of speed and performance as well as expectations of immediacy and accuracy that even the very best websites can't hope to compete with. And the competitive bar just keeps rising. The truth is that we're all suckers for speed and simplicity – save me time and make me more productive and I'm yours.

Today's reality is that websites are pretty much yesterday's news and the vast majority (to the extent that they haven't already been practically abandoned by their owners) are destined very shortly to be orphaned or consigned to the virtual dustbin. They're slow on a good day and too often plagued by latency issues; they're fundamentally static rather than interactive; far too many still aren't built or optimized for mobile use; and even the most conscientious webmasters can't really keep the data on these sites current because everything is changing way too fast. High velocity computing can rapidly supply the framework and the appropriate context for delivery, but that's not the same as effectively generating authentic and engaging content as opposed to rote and routine responses. And very frankly, adding a couple of widgets, a sidecar Twitter feed, or a few other flashy bells and whistles doesn't contribute anything much to the utility equation or to the perceived value of a visit. Too often searching the web these days is an exhausting and unproductive waste of time unless you know precisely what you're looking for.

And things aren't ever going to get better because all the positive movement and all the vectors are pointing in the wrong direction for anyone to even imagine a day when websites will once again matter. Mobile online use has convincingly overtaken the desktop and the usage gap is growing every quarter across all cohorts and age groups. In addition, and most strikingly, over 80% of the current mobile online use is now channeled opaquely through applications rather than overtly and transparently through browsers. This migration to mobile applications (and the closed-off connection conduits that they create) have created what I call the "App Gap" for Google because you can't measure and you certainly can't monetize what you can't see.

And the rapidly widening social gap is even more problematic for Google. The vast volume of meaningful traffic, the influential action and engaged activity, and ALL of the buzz and energy are focused today on social actions and sharing and not on search or research. Search is a sporadic, need-based and linear process. When it's done in the moment, it's done. Social is an emotional, expansive and ongoing sharing experience which is not only contagious, but exponential in that it grows and builds on itself. As a rule of thumb, and at least until you get burned or reach a certain age, the more you share, the more you're inclined to share in the future because you become increasingly psychologically invested in the process. Information may want to be free, but it turns out (no surprise here) that we want to be with our friends. There are a number of complex and powerful drivers behind these group and cohort-based behavioral changes, but one thing is abundantly clear – none of this is good news for Google.

As the novelty of "search" has worn off and the pure excitement of spontaneous exploration has dissipated, search has changed from a joy to just a job. It's an incidental and reflexive part of our day and nothing more. The more efficient and informed that search became; the less interesting and serendipitous it was. It was the triumph of the dispassionate engineers – all about dispatch and discipline (speed and results) with all the drama and passion of discovery being drained away. In a sense, Google did its job too well.

Today search is a heavily-manipulated mirror (reflecting back and confirming what we already know) rather than a window on new worlds. Among other critical differences from the much more intriguing Facebook interest graph approach is that in order to launch a Google search, you pretty much have to know where you're headed and you need create at least a modestly informed description of what you're looking for. The search box doesn't fill itself. It's not an adventure; it's a task. It's not a place we want to go these days; it's a place where we have to go when we need to accomplish some narrow and specific inquiry. The web today is about work, not wonder. And it's lonely out there as well because search is a solitary enterprise and we're all social animals.

The App Gap is just Google's latest problem as it struggles to continue to matter in a marketplace where the playing field has changed radically while Google's core offerings really haven't. Google needs to find a way into these new activity spaces, but many of its belated and reactive responses (and even its new and somewhat novel offerings) have fallen way short of the mark. Google was great when the web was about links, pages and anonymity. But when Facebook made it personal and the smart phone made it social and mobile, Google simply lost its way. You can't engineer emotions and you can't arbitrarily construct connections and engagement with others.

Shopping and social are where it's at today and, in those sectors, Google's become an also-ran. Maybe not quite as much of a yawn as Yahoo, but nothing to write home about for sure. Far more people search every day for products on Amazon than on Google even though its new Product Listing Ads (PLAs) are arguably better suited to mobile search than Amazon's offerings. The problem is no one knows they're there because no one sees them. And why is that? Because search isn't sexy or exciting any more. If there's one thing worse than being a chore or a commodity, it's being a tool or a utility. And the situation in the social sphere is even worse. Google+ has plenty of what I would characterize as "manufactured" members, but they're generally ghosts and they're not engaged with the service and – worst of all - they're simply not sharing. G+ has about 2% of the social sharing activity today while Facebook has over 50%, Twitter is at about 24% and LinkedIn and Pinterest account for another 19%.

If you don't have a substantial seat at the table, it's hard to have anything meaningful to say about the game or to the players. Without a window into Facebook's world; some perspective on Pinterest; or any idea of what's happening on Instagram, Twitter or

WhatsApp, it feels like Google's on the outside looking in and you have to wonder how much longer Google's advertising model will make sense to the major media and advertising buyers. If you're not where your advertisers' targets are spending their time and money, at the end of the day, you're nowhere.

SIMPLY STREAMING ... SUCKS

Please stop streaming stuff that sucks. No one cares. No one's watching. And, just because you can do it doesn't mean you should. And, as hard as it is to imagine, just because it happened to you doesn't make it interesting to us. You're constantly cluttering up the channels with your crap. And it seems like the spread of cheap video tools and technology isn't helping the situation – it's actually making it worse because now every clown with a camera can be a digital media publisher. Technology used without talent is less than a tool – it's a tragedy.

And even new innovations like *Hyperlapse* compression video which can speed up and smooth out the video viewing (without the shakes and constant jumping around) can't fix the presentation problem because when we're watching speakers (as opposed to road trips), there's no way to accelerate the accompanying (and obviously necessary) audio without sounding like Mickey Mouse. Media (or technology) that gets in the way of communication is less than useless.

UGC used to mean User Generated Content which contained – at least occasionally – some useful, meaningful and authentic material. Now, as far as the glut of webcasts which are indiscriminately spewing out massive amounts of video (and, frankly, podcasts aren't typically much better), it pretty much means Unwatchable Gratuitous Claptrap.

But it doesn't have to be that way if the makers would only take a few minutes (that's all anyone has anyway) to put themselves in the viewer's shoes. If we need help sleeping or want to be bored to death, there's always C-SPAN. And, as trite as it seems, we really do prefer quality over quantity - especially when you're asking us to commit our scarce time and – even more importantly – our attention to your offerings. It's not a volume game; it's not supposed to be a Friskies buffet; it's all about choice and value.

So next time you're getting ready to stream a talk or a panel or any other event, do us all a big favor and do these four critical things:

(1) Get a producer/director

A stream is NOT a show. Get a real producer/director (not a camera man or worse yet a tripod) who actually knows that not everything that everyone does or says during a program is worth capturing for posterity and who also knows the difference and can make intelligent choices. Get a second camera and a switcher and also (if there are slides or other presentation materials) get clean, legible digital copies of those materials as well. Incorporate the audience into the shoot. Make the visuals interesting and not static and use the zoom so we don't feel throughout the show that we got some of the worst seats in the house.

(2) Get an editor

The real value of these kinds of video-captured events isn't the few people who watch for a few minutes simultaneously online. They will generally get bored or go blind fairly quickly and bail out. If there's any lasting and archival value, it's in what use you make of the content after the fact. And to create intelligent, informative and useful content that someone will be willing to watch, you need an editor who knows the material, understands the goals, and can turn out the kind of product that you and your organization can be proud of. Vary the camera angles, intercut the slides, add some audience reactions, etc. It's not hard – it just takes some time and some thought. And it's a real talent also – not just something that people learn how to do. As Liz Taylor's 7th husband said: "I know what to do, but the challenge is to make it interesting."

(3) Give us the good stuff

Let the editor do his or her job. Cherry picking has gotten a bad name somehow, but we don't care to watch introductions that we can read, administrative announcements for the room (and we don't have to silence our cell phones), sponsor acknowledgments, or coming events calendars. Do you see where I'm going with this? Cut the crap and give us the beef – the good stuff – the 10% of the conversations that matters and from which we can learn something new. Content ultimately is cheap; wisdom is invaluable and worth watching.

(4) Give us a break

15 minutes of anything today is a lifetime. We're starting to see 7 second commercials for a reason. So decide early on what the outside time limit of your piece is going to be and then hold your editor to delivering the best material he can within those constraints. The best people will tell you that constraints encourage more creativity rather than the opposite as you might think. Think highlights and high value rather than heavy lifting. And respect the target audience's time above all.

When the dust settles, you want to be sending out something that people will want to see. Don't let your media get in the way of your message.

METRICS MATTER MORE THAN MOONSHOTS

Today, we have a much better and clearer view of where technology will take us over the next few years and how it will continue to significantly alter our lives. The primary focus – per my own personal crystal ball – will be on "efficacy" – products, services, systems, software and things that help us get other things done – more quickly and more economically. The overwhelming emphasis will be on saving us time, saving us money and making us more productive – these are the metrics that make for businesses that will consistently make their builders money as long as they continue to deliver the goods. Moonshots (literal or figurative) don't really matter in the Midwest – concrete results do.

I realize that simply shutting down the spam-spewing email systems of the world would make us all more effective, but I don't see that happening. I also don't expect to see many bionic anythings and I think we'll also have to wait quite a while for social robots and other intelligent household helpers. In fact, I wouldn't expect any dramatic advances or new "miracles" any time soon because the upcoming changes will most likely be both much more mundane and also tremendously more beneficial in ways that really matter to us. The next several generations of high-tech advances won't be about inventing new things - they will be about making the everyday objects we deal with in our day-to-day lives smarter, more responsive, and more helpful to us.

These developments will be driven by two (now fairly obvious) considerations: (1) every one of us is constantly connected to the Internet cloud by increasingly intelligent devices which will all compute; and (2) our basic expectations (which are forever growing and expanding) are that we will use these connected devices to provide us with what we need, when we need it, wherever we are, and without asking. This is the new world which we will come to call the Internet of Everything.

We'll make smarter choices every day about a wide variety of things based on vast quantities of better information which will be available all of the time in the palm of our hands. And many of the basic decisions which are required will be made quickly and automatically for us by high-velocity computers living somewhere in the cloud based on the unimaginable quantities of data being generated by every action we take, every move that we make, every venue we enter, and the trails of digital exhaust that we will leave behind wherever we go.

So what exactly are the kinds of things that we can reasonably expect to see today or in the near future? Things that will seem super cool tomorrow and which, by next year, we'll all take completely for granted.

Here are 3 categories of intelligent device-driven interactions that will become everyday parts of our lives.

(1) Who Are You Lookin' At?

The new Samsung phones turn off their screens when we aren't looking at them. New photo apps won't snap a picture if we're not smiling. Others won't take the shot until we signal them by making a fist. Our slabs and tabs are looking at us just as intently as we continue to study them.

(2) Who Are You Talkin' To?

New cloud-connected pill bottles will remind us to take our medications and just how much of each prescription we should be taking. New haptic utensils and clothes will vibrate to remind us to slow down when we're eating too fast and speed up when we're walking too slowly.

(3) What Are You Waitin' For?

Our phones (which we call mobile "trackers" that just happen to make calls) will alert merchants as we enter their stores to send us immediate, totally-personalized offers, specials and coupons on the way into the store when they're useful instead of wasting paper and trees printing long receipts that never even make it out of the grocery bags once we leave.

There are many more examples and these are just brief glimpses of the future. Exciting, challenging, and constantly changing. Buckle up.

ABOUT THE AUTHOR

Howard Tullman is the CEO of 1871 in Chicago where digital startups get their start. He is also the General Managing Partner of two venture funds: Chicago High-Tech Investment Partners and G2T3V, LLC, which both focus on funding disruptive innovators. He is the former Chairman and CEO of Tribeca Flashpoint Media Arts Academy in Chicago. He is an active member of numerous city, state and civic boards and organizations and a tireless supporter and mentor to many start-ups and other businesses and individuals. He has successfully founded more than a dozen high-tech businesses in his 50 year career and created more than $1 billion in investor value as well as thousands of new jobs. He writes a regular weekly blog on The Perspiration Principles for Inc. Magazine and can be directly contacted:

- by email at h@1871.com
- on twitter @tullman
- his blog: tullman.blogspot.com
- his primary website: www.tullman.com

To get all of Howard's blog posts in one download, visit Blogintobook.com/tullman/.